THE EXPLORER'S BIBLE

Volume 1: From Creation to the Exodus

Teacher's Lesson Plan Manual
By Rabbi Miriam T. Spitzer

24 Ready-to-Use Lesson Plans

Includes ways to use the Internet to deepen understanding, and to add creativity, interactivity, and excitement to your lessons

Project Editor: Yaffa Klugerman
Design: Jill A. Winitzer
Copyright © 2011 Behrman House, Inc.
Millburn, New Jersey
ISBN: 978-0-87441-933-7 • Manufactured in the United States of America

Behrman House, Inc.
www.behrmanhouse.com

CONTENTS

Introduction 3
  Talking About God 3
  Structure of the Textbook 3
  Structure of the Lesson Plans 4
  Group Work 4
  Differentiated Instruction 5
  Use of Technology 5
  Opening Rituals 6
  Bringing It Home 6

Essential Questions 7

Lesson Plans
  Chapter 1: The Birth of the World
    Lesson 1 8
    Lesson 2 9
  Chapter 2: Good and Evil in the Garden of Eden 10
  Chapter 3: My Brother's Keeper 11
  Chapter 4: The Man Who Walked with God 12
  Chapter 5: The Impossible Tower
    Lesson 1 13
    Lesson 2 14
  Chapter 6: Abraham Finds His Way
    Lesson 1 15
    Lesson 2 16
  Chapter 7: Abraham Speaks Up
    Lesson 1 17
    Lesson 2 18
  Chapter 8: The Sacrifice 19
  Chapter 9: Rebecca's Kindness 20
  Chapter 10: Twins, Tricks, and Trouble 21
  Chapter 11: Jacob's Discovery
    Lesson 1 22
    Lesson 2 23
  Chapter 12: Jacob's Struggle 24
  Chapter 13: The Dreamer 25
  Chapter 14: Joseph's Gift 26
  Chapter 15: Joseph's Forgiveness 27
  Chapter 16: Baby Moses 28
  Chapter 17: Moses Stands Before God 29
  Chapter 18: Freedom and the Future
    Lesson 1 30
    Lesson 2 31

Assessments 32

INTRODUCTION

Teaching Torah to children is a special joy and privilege, and *The Explorer's Bible* allows you and your students to enter the world of Torah study in a modern, accessible, and exciting way. It combines elements of our timeless tradition with a contemporary outlook and approach to personal growth and values. Through a rich and varied assortment of stories, discussion, and activities, *The Explorer's Bible* introduces students to the lifelong exploration of our most sacred text. In the process, they are encouraged to reflect on their personal values, goals, and relationships. Above all, they are encouraged to make the lessons of Torah a part of their own lives.

This manual provides teachers with ready-to-use lesson plans for every chapter of *The Explorer's Bible*. The lessons occasionally require some advance preparation; for example, gathering art supplies or printing a list of guided questions for discussion. You also may need to adapt the lesson plans for your specific situation. The basic plans, however, are all here.

TALKING ABOUT GOD

The Explorer's Bible is a book of Torah stories and God is a key character in the Torah. *The Explorer's Bible* does not shy away from some of the hard questions in the Torah, and students should see that their teachers take such questions very seriously and struggle with appropriate responses. The best way to teach *yirat shamayim*, reverence for God, is to model it. Questions about God and Torah should be encouraged in the classroom, as long as they are presented in a respectful manner.

STRUCTURE OF THE TEXTBOOK

The Explorer's Bible is divided into 18 chapters, which cover the text of the Torah from Genesis 1:1-Exodus 12:42. These chapters present the biblical account of creation and early human beings, the stories of the patriarchs and matriarchs, and the saga of the birth of the people of Israel as they left the oppression of Egypt.

The Explorer's Bible also contains the following recurring features, presented by cartoon "guides," which enrich the core text:

- **Time Traveler** challenges students to imagine that they are present at the time of the story—and to learn from biblical figures "firsthand."
- **Word Wizard** explores the meaning behind key Hebrew words and phrases.
- **Midrash Maker** introduces students to classical *midrashim* from rabbinic and other sources and invites students to create their own *midrashim*.
- **Wisdom Weavers** summarizes and reinforces the main theme of the chapter. Following each Wisdom Weavers is a visual activity that allows students to further explore the chapter's core concept.
- **Compass notes** in the margin expand on, explain, or propose questions based on the core text.

STRUCTURE OF THE LESSON PLANS

This Lesson Plan Manual includes 24 ready-to-use lesson plans of approximately 50 minutes each for *The Explorer's Bible Volume 1: From Creation to the Exodus*. It includes one lesson for 12 of the chapters and two lessons for six of the chapters.

Each lesson plan includes the following components:

- **Essential Question.** The overarching question of the lesson; usually, an open-ended question that lends itself to many different answers and to repeated examination over the course of a lifetime. Essential questions generally use lessons from the Torah to illuminate the students' own lives.
- **Learning Objectives.** A list of three main goals that the students will achieve by the end of the lesson.
- **Getting Started.** An opening activity, discussion or song that "hooks" the students in and sets the scene for what will follow.
- **Exploring the Text.** Opportunities to delve into the text using a combination of dramatic reading, reading in pairs, play acting, silent reading, and more. How the stories are read will vary not only from lesson to lesson, but also within the lessons themselves.
- **Experiential Learning.** Opportunities for students to learn by doing. Activities may include art projects, games, quizzes, play acting, and more.
- **The Tech Connection.** Suggestions for enhancing lessons through the use of technology, often using but not limited to the Internet. See Use of Technology on page 5 for more details.
- **Wrapping It Up.** A conclusion to the lesson, offering an opportunity to review and reflect on what was learned.

GROUP WORK

One principle of the religious school classroom should be that everyone works with everyone. That is part of the larger goal of teaching *derech eretz*, moral behavior. As such, groups should vary. While it might be tempting to place students who work well together in the same group, doing so will ultimately prevent students from developing the skills they need to work with all sorts of people. Teachers should make sure that over the course of time, everyone works with everyone: boys with girls, louder students with quieter students, and strong readers with weaker readers.

For the purpose of this manual, "small groups" means groups of three to four students. Sometimes the lesson calls for dividing the class in half or in three groups, rather than in small groups. Often the lesson calls for students to work in pairs. In most lessons, it will be advantageous to ensure that groups include diverse learners with diverse strengths. You may sometimes find it useful to divide into homogeneous groups or pairs.

At the beginning of the year, teachers should establish clear rules and expectations for group work. For example, students should be expected to speak with indoor voices and to remain within their groups. You may find it useful to have a delineation of jobs within the groups, so every student knows what his or her job is that day. (Note that not every job is necessarily applicable to every group work assignment.) Some possible jobs could include:

- Recorder: Takes notes on the group's discussions and ideas.
- Reporter: Reports the group's work to the class.
- Illustrator: Draws the group's ideas.
- Reader: Reads aloud to the group.
- Encourager: Encourages group members to stay on task.

DIFFERENTIATED INSTRUCTION

Always remember that we are not teaching text; we are teaching children. The mood we set in our classroom, the *derech eretz* expectations, and the relationships we build are at least as important as the material we are teaching.

Children learn in a variety of ways. Some students learn best by reading aloud, some by reading silently, and some by hearing the words read to them. Some students are visual learners, some are auditory learners, and some are kinesthetic learners. Some students learn best in groups and some prefer to work alone.

The lessons in this manual are designed to provide opportunities for different kinds of learning, both over time and within each lesson plan. While students should be encouraged to play to their strengths, they also should be encouraged to expand their comfort zone and explore other avenues of learning. Thus, not only should the skilled artists should participate in drawing activities, and not only the dramatic students should be involved in dramatic readings, but all students should be given opportunities to engage in all different kinds of activities.

Most of the lessons vary activities at least every 15 minutes or so. Doing so will keep children interested and involved in what is going on. Every lesson plan also includes at least one opportunity for **Experiential Learning**, meaning that students learn by doing. Such activities include quizzes, games, drama, art projects, creative writing, poetry writing, and more.

For suggestions on accommodating students with special needs, see *The Explorer's Bible Volume I: Teaching Guide,* page 8.

USE OF TECHNOLOGY

Technology offers a myriad of opportunities for enriching the learning experience. Many lesson plans include **The Tech Connection,** with suggestions for using the Internet to increase the excitement and interactivity of the lessons.

If you cannot use the Internet in your classroom, you can usually print out the information, pictures, and quizzes in advance to give to the students. Teachers may also opt to strengthen the home-school connection by sending home suggestions for enrichment using the Internet.

Keep in mind that technology should be a tool for learning rather than a goal in and of itself. Send students to only to Web sites that you have already visited and approved. One that is frequently used in this lesson plan manual is http://www.babaganewz.com/. This site is loaded with age-appropriate articles and games on the themes that we are exploring in *The Explorer's Bible*.

OPENING RITUALS

1. Consider posting a question on the blackboard or easel each day before the students arrive. When they enter the room, they should write their answers under the question. This may be a review question from the last time, the question they discussed with their families for homework (see **Bringing It Home** below), or some other Jewish question.
2. Students should bring their textbooks to their seats, ready to begin.
3. To emphasize that Torah study is a mitzvah, consider beginning each lesson with the blessing for Torah study.

בָּרוּךְ אַתָּה יהוה אֱלֹהֵינוּ מֶלֶךְ הָעוֹלָם, אֲשֶׁר קִדְּשָׁנוּ בְּמִצְוֹתָיו וְצִוָּנוּ לַעֲסוֹק בְּדִבְרֵי תוֹרָה.

Baruch Atah Adonai Eloheinu Melech ha'olam asher kidshanu b'mitzvotav v'tzivanu la'asok b'divrei Torah.

Praised are You, Adonai our God, Ruler of the world, who makes us holy with commandments and commands us to immerse ourselves in Torah study.

BRINGING IT HOME

Fostering a home-school connection is one key to success in Jewish education. Every lesson includes ideas that can easily be sent home for further discussion, particularly in **The Tech Connection.** Here are some ways to reinforce a regular home-school connection:

1. Write a question on the board every day to be discussed at home. Before the next class begins, students can write in answers or comments from their home discussion. Alternatively, this can be done on large sheets of paper on an easel and saved.
2. Maintain a class Web site or blog where the question related to the lesson is posted and students and families can share or discuss their answers.
3. Send home regular notes to parents with a discussion topic.

FINALLY...

The Talmud suggests that the greatest of *mitzvot* is "Talmud Torah," Torah study, because the study of Torah ultimately leads to all other *mitzvot*. May your teaching enrich you and your students with insights, learning, and the opportunities to perform many more *mitzvot* in the Jewish community and beyond. Enjoy!

(Portions of introduction adapted from *The Explorer's Bible Volume I: Teaching Guide*)

ESSENTIAL QUESTIONS

CHAPTER	PAGES	ESSENTIAL QUESTIONS
1 The Birth of the World	8-15	**Lesson 1:** *For what was God preparing the world?* **Lesson 2:** *What does it mean to be created* b'tzelem Elohim, *in the image of God?*
2 Good and Evil in the Garden of Eden	16-23	*How does knowing the difference between good and evil require us to behave?*
3 My Brother's Keeper (Cain and Abel)	24-29	*What does it mean to be our "brothers' keepers?"*
4 The Man Who Walked with God (Noah)	30-37	*How can we remain true to Jewish values and ideals despite the behavior of those around us?*
5 The Impossible Tower	38-43	**Lesson 1:** *What did the generation of the Tower of Babel do wrong?* **Lesson 2:** *What can we learn about the Tower of Babel from looking at art?*
6 Abraham Finds His Way	44-51	**Lesson 1:** *Why did God choose Abraham?* **Lesson 2:** *Why is God's promise to give the Land of Israel to Abraham's descendants important?*
7 Abraham Speaks Up	52-59	**Lesson 1:** *Should not the Judge of all the earth act justly?* **Lesson 2:** *How should we, like Abraham and Lot, speak up for justice?*
8 The Sacrifice (Akedah)	60-67	*Why does God give Abraham such a difficult test?*
9 Rebecca's Kindness	68-75	*What are Jewish ways of demonstrating* derech eretz?
10 Twins, Tricks, and Trouble (Jacob, Esau)	76-85	*What went wrong in Isaac and Rebecca's family and why?*
11 Jacob's Discovery	86-93	**Lesson 1:** *When and where do we feel God with us in our lives?* **Lesson 2:** *How does dishonesty lead to more dishonesty and how can we stop the spiral?*
12 Jacob's Struggle	94-101	*What does it mean to "struggle with God"?*
13 The Dreamer (Joseph)	102-109	*Was Jacob right in giving Joseph the k'tonet pasim?*
14 Joseph's Gift	110-119	*How can we use our own gifts and talents towards* tikun olam, *making the world a better place?*
15 Joseph's Forgiveness	120-129	*Is it more important to be right or to forgive people who have done us wrong?*
16 Baby Moses	130-137	*What can we do to help bring justice to the world for Jews and others?*
17 Moses Stands Before God	138-147	*How is the God of Abraham, the God of Isaac, the God of Jacob, also the God of each one of us?*
18 Freedom and the Future	148-157	**Lesson 1:** *Why do we observe Passover?* **Lesson 2:** *How is putting a mezuzah on our doorpost a choice that marks us as part of the Jewish community?*

CHAPTER 1

THE BIRTH OF THE WORLD
Lesson 1

Essential Question: For what was God preparing the world?

Lesson Objectives Students will be able to:
1. Recognize that "Genesis 1:1" is read as Genesis, chapter 1, verse 1.
2. Think of creation as a gradual process.
3. Read or chant the last line of each day in Hebrew (*vayehi erev...*)

Getting Started: (5 minutes)
Guided imagery. (See **Compass**, page 9.) Students close their eyes and imagine the world before there was a world. Speak softly. The world had "no shape and no form." As their eyes are closed, open and shut the lights or the shades for effect.

Exploring the Text: (10-15 minutes)
1. Teach the students to read Genesis 1:1-5 as: Genesis, Chapter 1, verses 1 through 5. Every heading with chapter and verse should be read the same way.
2. Explain that this is the very beginning of the Torah. A volunteer reads the first paragraph on page 9 aloud. Ask: Which day of the week was it? (*This is not as obvious as it sounds. It may not have occurred to students that this is describing the first Sunday.*) Which comes first, day or night? (*Night.*) Explain that this is the reason that Jewish days begin the evening before; for example, Shabbat begins Friday night. In the picture on page 8, which part depicts Sunday? (*The very center.*) What does the picture of Sunday show?

Experiential Learning: (20 minutes)
1. Divide the class into four groups. Assign each group a day of the week, Monday through Thursday. (We will do Friday and Shabbat in the next lesson.) Allow time for each group to read what was created on their day and to examine the picture on page 8.
2. Bring the class back together. Call out: Sunday! The entire class reads together: "And there was evening, and there was morning, the first day." Write on the board in Hebrew:
וַיְהִי עֶרֶב וַיְהִי בֹקֶר יוֹם אֶחָד (*Vayehi erev, vayehi boker, yom eḥad*). Teach the class to read the verse in Hebrew, and if you are comfortable doing so, to chant it as in the synagogue on Simḥat Torah.
3. For days Monday through Thursday:

    a. Call out the name of the day.

    b. The group assigned that day explains what was created, using the illustration as a guide.

    c. The class reads together, "And there was evening, and there was morning..."

    d. Write in Hebrew: "*Vayehi erev, vayehi boker, yom...*" (*sheni*—Monday, *she'lishi*—Tuesday, *revii*—Wednesday, *hamishi*—Thursday). Point out that in Hebrew the days of the week do not have names; they have numbers.

Wrapping It Up: (5 minutes)
Reflection. What was created first? (*Heaven and earth.*) What was created by the end of Thursday? (*Sky, dry land, seas, plants, sun, moon, stars, fish, birds.*) What was missing? (*Animals and people.*) For what was God preparing the world? (*People.*) What did God see (almost) every day? (*That it was good.*)

Chapter 1: Lesson 2
Essential Question: What does it mean to be created *b'tzelem Elohim*, in the image of God?

Lesson Objectives Students will be able to:
1. Explain the concept of *b'tzelem Elohim*.
2. Give examples of how we act *b'tzelem Elohim* in the world.
3. Demonstrate how observing Shabbat is an example of acting *b'tzelem Elohim*.

Getting Started: (5 minutes)
1. Using the picture on page 8, quickly review the days of creation that have been learned so far. Look at the final ring. What do we think will be created on Friday? *(Animals.)* What else do we think will be created on Friday that is not in the picture? *(People.)* What day of the week is missing from the picture? *(Shabbat.)*

Exploring the text: (10 minutes)
1. Page 12. Genesis 1:24-31. A volunteer reads the first three lines out loud until: "God saw this was good." Ask: What was good? *(Creation, including the animals.)* Was it good enough? How do we know? *(It was not yet good enough; the very next words are "Then God said …" meaning that creation was not yet complete.)*
2. A student reads the next two sentences out loud. Students underline "in the image of God." Read the **Word Wizard** and make sure students understand what *b'tzelem Elohim* means.
3. A student reads to the end of the section out loud. See **Compass**, page 12. Discuss: Why does God see it as "very good?" *(Now there are people.)* What was different about the sixth day? *(Only now are there creations in God's image; only now are there people.)*

Experiential Learning: (20 minutes)
1. Time to Rest. To be done individually or in small groups, on separate sheets of paper:
    a. **Time Traveler**, page 13. Students draw a picture, compose a poem, or write a description of the first Shabbat.

    OR

    b. Students draw a picture, compose a poem, or write a description of themselves observing Shabbat.
2. **Self Portrait**, page 15. Emphasize the term *b'tzelem Elohim* even though it is not written on this particular page. Students draw a picture, compose a poem, or write a description of how they can use a tool to work *b'tzelem Elohim* to make the world a better place.

> **Wrapping It Up:** (10-15 minutes)
> Gather the papers and make a class collage of the class acting *b'tzelem Elohim*, with sections for weekdays and Shabbat. Reflection: Read page 14 together. What can we do on weekdays to show that we are created *b'tzelem Elohim*? *(Acting as partners with God to make the world a better place, working in the world, doing creative work, improving and protecting the world.)* On Shabbat? *(Refraining from creative work, not working, and resting like God rested.)*

CHAPTER 2: GOOD AND EVIL IN THE GARDEN OF EDEN — Lesson 1

Essential Question: How does knowing the difference between good and evil require us to behave?

Lesson Objectives Students will be able to:
1. Discuss what it means that human beings are to "work and tend" the earth.
2. Recount the consequences of Adam and Eve's disobedience.
3. Explain how the knowledge of good and evil affects the choices people must make.

Getting Started: (5 minutes)
Students think of a tough choice they have made recently. Ask: Why was the choice difficult? What were your options? How did you decide what to do? Do you think you made the right choice? Explain that the story of the Garden of Eden teaches us about the importance of making good choices.

Exploring the Text: (20 minutes)
1. A volunteer reads page 17, Genesis 2:4-15 aloud. Do **Midrash Maker**, page 19, in pairs or small groups. Begin by reading the Midrash Maker bubble aloud and explaining that a midrash is a story that, is while not actually in the Torah, explains something that is in the Torah or fills in a gap in the Torah story.
2. Students silently read Genesis 2:16-17. Ask: What was God's command? (*Not to eat from the Tree of Knowledge.*) To whom did God give the command? (*To the human who would soon be called Adam; the human who would soon be called Eve was not created yet, so she did not hear God's command directly.*)
3. Student partners read pages 18 and 20, Genesis 2:18-3:24. When they finish, ask: Who blamed whom in this story? (*Adam blamed the woman; the woman blamed the snake.*) How do you think that made God feel? (*Answers may include: frustrated, surprised, not surprised.*) Why is it wrong to blame others for our actions?

Experiential Learning: (10 minutes)
Switch partners and do **Time Traveler** on page 21.

The Tech Connection: (15 minutes)
Remind the class that it is our responsibility to work and tend the earth (see page 17.) There are many ways to fulfill that responsibility and we are going to learn about some of them now. Switch partners or combine into small groups. Go to http://www.babaganewz.com/values/protecting-the-environment. Choose one of the many options having to do with protecting the environment and read it together.

> **Wrapping It Up:** (5 minutes)
> Read and discuss **Wisdom Weavers**, page 22. How does knowing the difference between good and evil require us to behave?

CHAPTER 3
MY BROTHER'S KEEPER
Lesson 1

Essential Question: What does it mean to be our "brothers' keepers?"

Lesson Objectives Students will be able to:
1. Tell the story of Cain and Abel, including possibilities of why they fought.
2. Define what it means to be a "brother's keeper" and provide examples of how to accomplish this.
3. Understand that Judaism requires us to be our brothers' keepers.

Getting Started: (2-3 minutes)
Students look at the picture on page 24 and describe each person.

Exploring the Text:
1. (5 minutes) The class reads Genesis 4:1-5 on page 25. Ask: Why do you think God accepted Abel's sacrifice and not Cain's? (*Students might point out that Abel brought meat, while Cain brought fruit. If this comes up, affirm that this is a legitimate answer, but explain that gifts of fruit and even grain were accepted in the Temple. Another response is that Abel brought the best of what he had, while Cain just brought whatever was available.*)
2. (5 minutes) Either as a class or individually, read the final three sections in the chapter.
3. (10 minutes) Write on the board: "Cain said to his brother Abel ...and when they were in the field, Cain set upon his brother Abel and killed him" (Genesis 4:8, New JPS Translation). Explain that the Torah does not describe the conversation between Cain and Abel. Student pairs write possible dialogues between Cain and Abel, which are presented to the class.
4. (5 minutes) Choose a Cain and an Abel to read **Midrash Maker**, page 27. According to this midrash, what were Cain and Abel fighting over? *(Property)* Explain that this is the beginning of a midrash which also suggests that Cain and Abel might have been fighting over religion or women.

Experiential Learning: (20 minutes)
1. Cain says to God, "Am I my brother's keeper?" Write on the board: הֲשֹׁמֵר אָחִי אָנֹכִי (*hashomer aḥi anochi*). Explain: "אח" (*aḥ*) means brother. Ask: What did Cain mean when he said *hashomer aḥi anochi*? (*He meant: Am I responsible for where my brother is or for what he does?*) Was Cain responsible for where Abel was at the time? (*Yes, he knew that he had already killed him.*)
2. Students complete the word search on page 29. Ask: Of the words included here, which three would you most want to be known for?
3. Discuss: What Jewish mitzvot demonstrate that we are our brothers' keepers? (*Answers might include: hospitality, tzedakah, visiting the sick, feeding the hungry, etc.*)

Wrapping It Up: (5 minutes)
The class together reads **Wisdom Weavers**, page 28. Students turn to pages 158 and 159 to see the overview of Who's Who in the beginning of the Torah. Point out that this is the first, but by no means the last, time we are going to hear about trouble between brothers in the book of Genesis.

CHAPTER 4
THE MAN WHO WALKED WITH GOD Lesson 1

Essential Question: How can we remain true to Jewish values and ideals despite the behavior of those around us?

Lesson Objectives Students will be able to:
1. Define the term "covenant" and identify the rainbow as the symbol of God's covenant with Noah.
2. Recount how Noah shows the courage of his convictions.
3. Describe ways a person can "walk with God."

Getting Started: (7 minutes)
Teach the students the blessing upon seeing a rainbow:

בָּרוּךְ אַתָּה אדני אֱלוֹהֵינוּ מֶלֶךְ הָעוֹלָם זוֹכֵר הַבְּרִית וְנֶאֱמָן בִּבְרִיתוֹ וְקַיָּם בְּמַאֲמָרוֹ

Barukh atah Adonai Eloheinu melech ha'olam zoher habrit vene'eman bivrito v'kayam b'ma'amaro.

Blessed is the Eternal our God, Ruler of universe, who remembers the covenant and is faithful to the covenant, and keeps God's promise.

Exploring the Text: (20 minutes)
1. A volunteer reads the first section out loud on page 31, Genesis 6:5-9. Ask: What does it mean to walk with God? *(To behave in a Godly fashion, to act as God wants people to act.)*
2. A student reads the bottom **Compass** defining "covenant." Students write the word בְּרִית *(brit)* in their books.
3. Students read pages 31 and 32, Genesis 6:14-22, 7:6-23, and 7:24-8:9, in pairs.
4. Students do **Time Traveler** on page 33 individually. After completing it, students exchange books and read each other's responses.
5. Students complete the story on page 35 and do pages 37 and 34 individually or in pairs.

Experiential Learning: (13 minutes)
1. Read **Wisdom Weavers**, page 36, as a class.
2. The class brainstorms some kind of difficult situation that students might encounter in their lives where "everyone" is doing something wrong, and students act out potential responses. Alternatively, break the class into groups to act out responses to these scenarios: The teacher leaves the class alone for a couple of minutes, telling the class to sit quietly. Everyone is talking loudly. What should you do? At lunch in school, everyone is making fun of the new kid. What should you do? You have money in your pocket that you were supposed to give to tzedakah, but everyone else is buying candy from the vending machine at recess. What should you do?

Wrapping It Up: (5 minutes)
Review the concept of *b'tzelem Elohim*, in the image of God. Discuss: How is being created *b'tzelem Elohim* related to walking with God? *(They are very similar ideas; in both cases we behave in a Godly way.)* Why do we say the rainbow blessing? *(To remind us of God's covenant with Noah, to remind us to walk with God as Noah did.)*

CHAPTER 5
THE IMPOSSIBLE TOWER
Lesson 1

Essential Question: What did the generation of the Tower of Babel do wrong?

(Note: The Torah does not tell us what the people did wrong and rabbinic answers abound, including that they wanted to see God, or even that they wanted to be God. One midrash suggests that the tower got so tall that it took a year to reach the top. If a worker fell off the tower, no one cared, but if a brick fell, everyone wept because it would take a full year to replace. The people stopped caring about people. Rabbi Yeshayahu Leibowitz suggests that the problem was totalitarianism: Working together for a common project is all well and good, until all individualism is forcibly suppressed, and that is what the people did wrong.)

Lesson Objectives Students will be able to:
1. Describe different opinions of what the builders of the Tower of Babel did wrong.
2. Articulate how the different approaches teach us different things about how we should behave.
3. Connect the words: *sham, shem, shamayim*.

Getting Started: (5 minutes)
Ask: Before the flood, what did the people do wrong? *(The Torah says that the land was full of "hamas," violence. On page 31, our text says "wicked deeds." These might include theft, lying, cheating, bullying each other, and being cruel. Note that after the flood, people worked together as a team. What is good about that? What might be bad about that? Answers might include that people can work together as a team to do something wrong or illegal.)*

Exploring the Text: (10 minutes)
Students read the story of the Tower of Babel on pages 39-40 to themselves and write down what they think the people did wrong.

Experiential Learning: (20 minutes)
There are a variety of children's stories about the Tower of Babel. Examples include *Mabel and the Tower of Babel* by John Ryan and *Does God Have a Big Toe? Stories About Stories in the Bible*, by Marc Gellerman. After the students have read the story from *The Explorer's Bible*, provide children's book versions of the story for them to read in small groups. Students keep a list of what the different stories imply that the people did wrong and how the stories teach us to behave.

The Tech Connection: (10 minutes)
In a dictionary or online, students look up the word "onomatopoeia." What are some examples? How is this related to the Babel story? See the **Compass** on page 40.

> **Wrapping It Up:** (10 minutes)
> The class together reads **Word Wizard** on page 40. Ask: Did any of the stories they read talk about the people trying to reach *shamayim*? Can we reach God by building skyscrapers?

Chapter 5: Lesson 2

Essential Question: What can we learn about the Tower of Babel from looking at art?

Lesson Objectives Students will be able to:
1. Explore "visual midrash."
2. Appreciate a different way of expressing/studying Torah.
3. Know that the Tower of Babel was imagined very differently in different times and places.

Note: The Tower of Babel has been explored in art in every generation. Students are fascinated by different renditions of the tower. Excellent examples from different times and places include:

1. http://en.wikipedia.org/wiki/The_Tower_of_Babel_%28Bruegel%29. Peter Bruegel the elder, 1563. (two paintings)
2. http://www.worldofescher.com/gallery/A60.html. Escher, 1928.
3. http://www.gettyimages.com/detail/51240551/Hulton-Archive. France, 1423.
4. http://www.safrai.com/details.php?id=440. David Sharir, 1975.
5. http://www.flickr.com/photos/44124368926@N01/3656982287

Getting Started: (5 minutes)
Choose one visual representation of the Tower of Babel and show it on the computer screen or on an overhead projector. Ask: What is this a picture of?

Exploring the Text: (5 minutes)
As a whole group, do a quick review of the Tower of Babel story from last class.

Experiential Learning:
1. (10 minutes) Explain to the class that no one knows what the Tower of Babel actually looked like, so artists are free to use their imaginations when they wish to paint pictures of the Tower. Every artist has a different vision, and we can learn different things from the different visions. Discuss the displayed picture using the following guided questions: What do you notice about the picture? What does the picture remind you of or make you think of? At what point in the story does the picture take place? What kinds of colors does it use and how does it make you feel? What do you think the artist was trying to say about the Tower of Babel? Was there anything else that the artist was trying to say? When you are comparing pictures, add: How are the two pictures like each other? How are they different?
2. (10 minutes) Provide worksheets with guided questions and "hard copies" of Tower of Babel pictures. Allow students to choose two pictures to explore. Students, in small groups or individually, compare and discuss the pictures using the guided questions. Some students may want to continue doing this with another picture or two.
3. (10 minutes) Provide art materials and encourage students to draw their own interpretations of the story, while thinking of the questions they asked about the art they saw. Alternatively, provide building materials such as blocks or popsicle sticks for students to construct a Tower of Babel.

Wrapping It Up: (5-10 minutes)
Come back together as a class. Ask students what they liked about this experience. Discuss how today's lesson was Torah study, even though we never opened a book at all. How did the art enrich our understanding of Torah?

CHAPTER 6
ABRAHAM FINDS HIS WAY
Lesson 1

Essential Question Why did God choose Abraham?

Lesson Objectives Students will be able to:
1. Identify the two promises God made to Abraham: that his descendants would become a great nation and that God would give them the land of Israel.
2. Explain how Abraham's treatment of family members (Lot) and guests can serve as a model for us today.
3. Define the term: *hachnasat orḥim*.

Getting Started: (5 minutes)
Play Debbie Friedman's "*L'chi Lach.*" Lyrics and recording can be found at http://www.lyricsmode.com/lyrics/d/debbie_friedman/lchi_lach.html and http://www.lyrics007.com/Debbie%20Friedman%20Lyrics/L%27chi%20Lach%20Lyrics.html. Play the song without comment. (We will discuss it at the end.)

Exploring the Text: (20 minutes)
1. Tell the students that this chapter comes from the *parashah* in the Torah called *Lech Lecha*.
2. For page 45, Genesis 11:26-12:7, select students to read the parts of the narrator and God for a dramatic reading. After completing the section, ask: What are the promises God made to Abraham? *(God will make Abraham a great nation, God will bless Abraham, God will give Canaan/Israel to Abraham's descendants forever.)* Write these on the board.
3. Summarize Genesis 13:1-7 briefly for the students.
4. Continue dramatic reading for Genesis 13:8-16, with room for extemporaneous additions. Choose a narrator, Abraham, and Lot—who will invent his own lines, as none are given. Why did Abraham give Lot the first choice of living spaces?
5. Continue dramatic reading for Genesis 17:1-18:16. Select students to play the narrator, God, and Abraham. Choose students to play Sarah and the guests, who will need to invent their own lines.
6. Read the **Compass** on page 48. How did Abraham practice the Jewish value of *hachnasat orḥim*, welcoming guests? How can we do the same?
7. Summarize Genesis 21:1-6 briefly for the class.

Experiential Learning: (15-20 minutes)
1. Ask: What kind of person was Abraham? How did he behave? *(Answers might include: He was obedient to God, generous to Lot, hospitable.)* List answers on the board.
2. Divide students into groups. Read **Midrash Maker** on page 49. Ask: What do we learn about Abraham from this midrash? What kind of a person was he and what kind of choices did he make? Add answers to the list on the board.
3. Students create their own *midrashim*, which should be written, illustrated, and displayed.

> **Wrapping It Up:** (5 minutes)
> Play Debbie Friedman's "*L'chi Lach*" again. Distribute lyrics to the students. Ask: Now that you have learned the story of Abraham, how do you like the song? When do you think would be a good time to sing it?

Chapter 6: Lesson 2

Essential Question: Why is God's promise to give the Land of Israel to Abraham's descendants important?

Lesson Objectives Students will be able to:
1. Identify God's promise to Abraham.
2. Trace God's promise through Jacob and Moses.
3. Connect the promise to the modern day State of Israel.

Getting Started: (5 minutes)

Play http://www.youtube.com/watch?v=6ZDSBF5xtoo, which shows David Ben Gurion announcing the birth of the State of Israel on May 14, 1948. The video is original footage, less than three minutes, and in Hebrew with English subtitles.

Exploring the Text: (10 minutes)
1. Ask students to skim chapter 6 and look for the times that God blesses Abraham with the land of Israel. Students underline the promise when they find it. *(Bottom of pages 45 and 46.)*
2. Students turn to page 88. Tell the class that Jacob was Abraham's grandson. Students find and underline God's promise in the middle of the page.
3. Students turn to the top of page 142, where God is speaking to Moses at the burning bush. Students underline God's promise.

Experiential Learning: (5-10 minutes)

Play Israeli Mail to familiarize students with names of places in Israel.
1. Students sit in chairs placed in a circle, with one person, the "*shaliaḥ*" or "*shliḥah*" (messenger), standing in the middle.
2. The *shaliaḥ/shliḥah* calls out: "I have a letter from city (x) to city (y)."
3. The two students whose cities are called must switch seats before the *shaliaḥ/shliḥah* can take one of their chairs.
4. To make the game a little more exciting, the *shaliaḥ/shliḥah* can occasionally call "e-mail!" and all the players must switch seats.
5. Variation: Provide pictures of the places and have the students hold the pictures during the game, thus familiarizing themselves not only with the place names, but also with images of places in Israel.

The Tech Connection: (15 minutes)

Students work in groups of two or three to identify locations on a map of Jerusalem. Go to http://www.babaganewz.com/activities/jerusalem-interactive-map. Students try to find:
1. A place where you could pray (*#15 Mount Scopus-Hecht Synagogue; #22 Kotel*)
2. A gate to the Old City (*#18 Jaffa Gate; #21 Zion Gate; #25 Damascus Gate*)
3. A place where you might go shopping (*#12 Machane Yehudah; #13 Ben Yehudah Street; #20 Cardo; #24 Arab shuk*)
4. A place having to do with transportation (*#1 Ben Gurion Airport; #3 Central Bus station*)
5. A place where you might go just for fun (*#9 Teddy Stadium and the Biblical Zoo*)

> **Wrapping It Up:** (10 minutes)
> *Discuss: Why is God's promise to give the Land of Israel to Abraham's descendants important?*

CHAPTER 7 ABRAHAM SPEAKS UP
Lesson 1

Essential Question: Should not the Judge of all the earth act justly?

Lesson Objectives Students will be able to:
1. Articulate that justice is a critical Jewish value.
2. Consider the role of God in the justice of the world.
3. Compare and contrast Abraham's behavior with that of Noah.
4. Define the words: *mishpat, tzedek,* tzaddik, tzedakah.

Getting Started: (5 minutes)
Look up the words *mishpat, tzedek,* tzaddik, and tzedakah in the dictionary and write down the definitions. What is the connection between those ideas? How is tzedakah an act of justice? *(Tzedek means justice. Tzedakah, giving money to those who need it, is closely tied to the idea of justice in the world. Likewise a tzaddik is a righteous person, which means a person who helps to increase justice in the world. Mishpat also means justice, and that is the word that Abraham uses here.)*

Exploring the Text: (5-10 minutes)
1. Students read the first three sections (Genesis 18:20-32) of the chapter.
2. Skip the sections about Lot. (We will come back to them in the next lesson.)
3. Students read the final section of the chapter, Genesis 19:27-29.

Experiential Learning: (20 minutes) Mini-bibliodrama.
1. Set the scene. Students imagine that they are Abraham speaking with God on a hot day. Ask: How do you (Abraham) feel when God tells you of a plan to destroy the cities of Sodom and Gemorrah? Students answer in the first person: "I feel ..." After several students answer, ask: How do you feel when God responds, "I will not destroy the city for the sake of the ten?" How do you feel when you wake up in the morning and see the smoke rising from the cities?
2. Reset the scene. Students imagine that they are Noah. Ask: How do you feel when God tells you there is going to be a flood and you have to build an ark? Students respond in the first person: "I feel ..." Ask: How do you feel when God tells you of a plan to destroy the world? How do you feel knowing that God is saving you and your family?
3. Two student volunteers act out a conversation between Noah and Abraham meeting one day in heaven. Switch volunteers.
4. Debrief. What did you (the student) think of what Noah/Abraham said?

The Tech Connection: (10 minutes)
Google the term "*tzedek.*" Make a list of the first ten organizations that appear and what they do. How many different kinds of organizations and kinds of justice did you find? (This can be done at home instead.)

> **Wrapping It Up:** (10-15 minutes)
> How does being created *b'tzelem Elohim* relate to Abraham's demand that the Judge of the world behave justly? *(Abraham is telling God that people are going to follow God's example, so God must set a good one.)*

Chapter 7: Lesson 2

Essential Question: How should we, like Abraham and Lot, speak up for justice?

Lesson Objectives Students will be able to:
1. Recognize that Lot, like Abraham, performed the mitzvah of *hachnasat orḥim*.
2. Discuss how the story of Sodom and Gemorrah teaches us to stand up for justice *(tzedek/mishpat)*. Abraham spoke up to God; Lot defied the people of his town.
3. Identify ways that we can stand up for justice.

Getting Started: (3 minutes)
Review the mitzvah of *hachnasat orḥim*, performed by Abraham and Sarah in the previous chapter and by Lot in this chapter.

Exploring the Text: (7 minutes)
Pairs take turns reading the final four sections of this chapter on pages 55 and 56.

The Tech Connection: (5 minutes per student or student pair.)
Quiz: What kind of courage do you possess? http://www.babaganewz.com/quizzes/are-you-a-creature-of-courage. Students take the quiz individually or in student pairs. If there are not enough available computers, print the quiz for students to complete in writing. To score, take the quiz yourself three times, being careful to indicate the same types of answers each time and print the three different possible conclusions. Make sure to print the support texts for each as well. Possible conclusions are Lone Wolf (stick to your own values); Galloping Gazelle (strength in numbers); and Roaring Lion (ready to confront authority). It will not be hard to look over the students' quizzes and see in which category each falls.

Experiential Learning:
1. (15 minutes) Small groups design skits where someone may or may not speak up or speak out. They may have ideas for skits from the situations given in the quiz. Other suggestions include:

    a. Your friends don't want to include the new kid at the lunch table.

    b. Two kids in the class make lots of noise when the teacher goes out for a couple of minutes. The teacher hears the noise in the hall and angrily keeps the whole class in for recess.

    c. Your grandmother gives you and your older brother $25.00 each for Hanukkah, but the envelope for your younger sister contains only $5.00.

2. (5 minutes) Pair up the groups. One group performs its skit for the other group in the pair.
3. (5 minutes) The spectator group performs its skit for the first group.

> **Wrapping It Up:** (5-10 minutes)
> Ask: How did Abraham stand up for justice? *(He argued with God, he divided up the land with Lot, he showed hospitality.)* How did Lot stand up for justice? *(The people of Sodom wanted to abuse the strangers that were visiting their town, and Lot would not let them.)* How should we stand up for justice? Tell the students that we will be learning about more people who stood up for justice, both in the Torah and in our own day.

CHAPTER 8

THE SACRIFICE
Lesson 1

Essential Question: Why does God give Abraham such a difficult test?

Lesson Objectives Students will be able to:
1. Describe how Abraham responded to God's test.
2. Define the term "Akedah" and identify the holiday on which the Akedah is read.
3. Explain the use of the shofar, what it reminds us to do, and its connection to the Akedah.

Getting Started: (5 minutes)
1. List on the board the challenges that Abraham has faced in his life so far. *(Answers may include: He was commanded to move to Canaan, he argued with God about Sodom and Gemorrah, he was childless for many years.)* Tell the class that now Abraham is about to face the greatest challenge of his life.
2. Students look at the picture on page 60. Ask: Where do you think the father and son in the picture are going?

Exploring the Text: (15 minutes) Dramatic reading.
1. Assign the following parts: **Compass** reader, narrator, God, Abraham, Isaac, angel of God, and Word Wizard.
2. The compass reader reads the **Compass** on the top of page 61.
3. Students with the parts of Abraham, God, and narrator read Genesis 22:1-2 on page 61.
4. The student assigned to **Word Wizard** reads the part on page 62. Discuss briefly.
5. Return to page 61 for a dramatic reading of Genesis 22:3-5 and Genesis 22:6-8 on page 62.
6. Students examine the picture on page 63. Ask: What do you notice about this picture? *(It is made up of little squares. Explain what a mosaic is and point out that the characters are labeled, and the colors are red-browns.)*
7. Students continue dramatic reading of Genesis 22:9-13 on page 64.
8. **Compass** reader reads **Compass** on page 64. Ask: Why did God test Abraham in this way? What does the story teach us? *(There are no easy answers, but perhaps God was trying to teach us that human sacrifice is abhorrent.)*

Experiential Learning: (10-15 minutes)
1. Students complete **Midrash Maker** on page 65 individually, followed by the crossword puzzle on page 67. Teacher circulates in the room, giving aid where needed.
2. When most students have completed the **Midrash Maker**, bring the class back together to read *midrashim* aloud.

Wrapping It Up: (5 minutes)
Read **Wisdom Weavers**, page 66. Discuss why we sound the shofar on Rosh Hashanah.

Tech Connection: (10 minutes)
See http://www.youtube.com/watch?v=GyHNKqmr-R8&feature=related for how to blow a shofar. If possible, allow students to practice on a real shofar.

CHAPTER 9
REBECCA'S KINDNESS
Lesson 1

Essential Question: What are Jewish ways of demonstrating *derech eretz*?

Lesson Objectives Students will be able to:
1. Describe how Abraham and Isaac responded to Sarah's death.
2. Identify at least three ways in which Rebecca showed kindness.
3. List ways we can follow Rebecca's example by practicing *derech eretz*.

Getting Started: (5 minutes)
Read **Wisdom Weavers** on page 74. Make a list on the board of Jewish ways to show *derech eretz*. When possible, include Hebrew terms. *(Examples might include: hospitality/hachnasat orḥim; respect for parents and teachers; standing up for justice like Abraham and Lot.)* Note: *Derech eretz* and acting *b'tzelem Elohim* are not precisely identical, but they are overlapping ideas, as is the notion of walking with God that we saw in the Noah chapter. In this chapter, Rebecca's kindness is used as an example of *derech eretz*.

Exploring the Text: (25 minutes) Dramatic reading.
1. Assign the following parts: Narrator, Abraham, Hittite spokesperson, second narrator, Eliezer, Rebecca, **Word Wizard**, third narrator, Laban, and Isaac. Students act out the story as they read. Sections will be interspersed with short discussions.
2. Dramatic reading, page 69, Genesis 23:1-19. Ask: What did Abraham do that was an example of *derech eretz*? *(He took care of Sarah after she died and buried her.)* Add caring for the dead to the *derech eretz* list on the board.
3. Dramatic reading, Genesis 24:1-7; Genesis 24:10-14; Genesis 24:15-21. Ask: What did Rebecca do that showed kindness and were examples of *derech eretz*? *(She offered Eliezer water; she drew water for the animals.)* Add generosity or kindness to strangers and feeding or caring for animals to the *derech eretz* list on the board.
4. Dramatic reading, Genesis 24:22-27. Ask: What else did Rebecca do that was an example of both kindness and *derech eretz*? *(She offered hospitality to Eliezer and his camels.)* Add hospitality to the *derech eretz* list, if it is not already there.
5. Finish the chapter with dramatic reading.

Experiential Learning: (10 minutes)
Students play the *derech eretz* game on page 75 in small groups.

The Tech Connection: (5 minutes)
Look up Rabbi Abraham Joshua Heschel. Who was he? List three to four things that he did in his life. Include at least two examples of either *derech eretz* or acting *b'tzelem Elohim* in his life.

> **Wrapping It Up:** (5 minutes)
> Rabbi Abraham Joshua Heschel said, "When I was young, I admired clever people. Now that I am old, I admire kind people." What do you think he meant by that? Do you agree with him?

CHAPTER 10 TWINS, TRICKS, AND TROUBLE
Lesson 1

Essential Question: What went wrong in Isaac and Rebecca's family and why?

Lesson Objectives Students will:
1. Describe the conflicts and tensions among the members of Isaac and Rebecca's family.
2. Empathize with/imagine how the Torah characters were feeling and why they might have made the choices that they made.
3. Create personal *midrashim* that build on the story.

Getting Started: (3 minutes)
Quick review. Ask: Who was Sarah married to? *(Abraham)*. What was their son's name? *(Isaac)* Who was Isaac married to? *(Rebecca.)* What do we know about Rebecca? *(She was kind; she offered water and shelter to Eliezer and his camels. She was brave; she came back with the servant to marry a stranger in a strange place.)*

Exploring the Text: (15 minutes)
Read the chapter in pairs.

Experiential Learning:
1. (15 minutes) Creative group work. (Each group will complete only one project, though the same project may be assigned to more than one group.)
    a. **Midrash Maker**, page 80. Three to four students create a midrash explaining why Esau was willing to sell his birthright in the words of both brothers.
    b. **Compass**, page 81. Two or three students think of three reasons why Isaac might have suspected a trick. Imagine that Isaac was talking to himself, trying to decide what to do. What would he have said?
    c. It was the night after the blessing and Isaac and Rebecca were alone in the tent. Two students write a dialogue between the parents. What does each say to the other?
    d. **Compass**, page 82. Three to four students thinks of the last time in the Torah when one sibling was jealous of another. How did that story end? How do you think this story will end? Write down thoughts.
2. (5 minutes) Discuss: What was Isaac and Rebecca's family like?
3. (5 minutes) Depending on size of class and number of groups, each group either shares its story with the whole class or with another group that had a different project.

Wrapping It Up: (7 minutes)
Time Traveler, page 83. Teacher reads the first word bubble and asks, "Who might have said this?"—then throws a beanbag to a student. The student must quickly answer who might have said it and why, and then throws the beanbag to a classmate. The classmate gives a second answer and throws the beanbag back to the teacher. Repeat for each word bubble.

The Tech Connection:
At home, students do **Compass**, page 77. In the Bible, people's names often describe them in some way. What is your Hebrew name? Look up what it means. Look up what your English name means. Do they mean the same thing?

CHAPTER 11 JACOB'S DISCOVERY
Lesson 1

Essential Question: When and where do we feel God with us in our lives?

Lesson Objectives Students will be able to:
1. Recount the story of Jacob from birth until his dream of angels going up and down a ladder.
2. Relate how Jacob's dream fit into his life.
3. Reflect on places and times that we might find God in our lives.

Getting Started: (10 minutes)
Students illustrate places or occasions where they feel that God is with them.

Exploring the Text: (15 minutes)
1. A volunteer reads the first two sentences on page 87. Ask: Why does Rebecca think Esau wants to kill Jacob?
2. Ask the class to quickly review Jacob's life until now. *(He is the younger twin, born holding his brother's heel; a quiet man who liked to stay home; his mother's favorite son; he bought the birthright from Esau; he tricked his father into giving him the blessing first; Esau threatened to kill him.)*
3. Volunteer reads to the end of the paragraph. Ask: Why does Rebecca want Jacob to go to Haran? *(To let Esau calm down.)* Why does Isaac want Jacob to go to Haran? *(To find a wife.)* Do you think Jacob wants to go to Haran? *(Answers will vary; the Torah does not tell.)*
4. Paint the picture for the class: Jacob is all alone, for maybe the first time in his life. He has no one with him—not his mom, his dad, his brother, a friend, nor a servant. He is traveling very far. It is the first night. He lies down on the ground to sleep, and then he has a dream. What do you think he might dream about?
5. A volunteer reads Genesis 28:11-16 on page 88.

Experiential Learning: (15 minutes)
1. Students illustrate Jacob's dream. While drawing, discuss: What do you think this dream actually was about? What was God telling Jacob? How do you think Jacob felt when he woke up from his dream? *(Answers may include comforted, reassured, happy, relieved, surprised.)* The commentators point out that one reason for Jacob's surprise may have been that he did not know that God would go with him outside of the land of Israel.
2. Read **Word Wizard**, page 88.

> **Wrapping It Up:** (10 minutes)
> Make a class bulletin board with two sections. One section should be titled: "BaMakom HaZeh" ("in this place") and should show places and times where the class feels God to be with them (illustrations from "Getting Started" above). One section should be titled "Jacob's Dream" and should show the class's different visions of what Jacob's dream looked like (illustrations from experiential learning above). Discuss: What Jewish rituals do we practice every day to help bring God into our lives? *(Answers may include: Saying* brachot *before we eat or when we see a rainbow, or wearing a* kippah *reminding us that God is above. Add here that acting* b'tzelem Elohim *and behaving with* derech eretz *are also ways to get closer to God.)*

The Explorer's Bible Volume I • Teacher's Lesson Plan Manual

Chapter 11: Lesson 2

Essential Question: How does dishonesty lead to more dishonesty and how can we stop the spiral?

Lesson Objectives Students will be able to:
1. Understand the story of Jacob marrying Leah and Rachel from different perspectives.
2. Explain how Jacob's dishonesty led to more dishonesty.
3. Know how to stop the spiral of dishonesty.

Getting Started: (10 minutes)
To discuss the effects of dishonest behavior, present this scenario: You are watching two children, Ariel and Randi, play marbles. You notice that Ariel is moving the marbles when Randi is not watching. Ask students: How does this make you feel about Ariel? Would you want to play marbles or any other game with Ariel? Do you think it would be fair if Randi also started cheating at marbles?

Exploring the Text: (7 minutes)
Students read the rest of the story on pages 89-90 individually.

Experiential Learning: (23 minutes)
1. Divide the students into three groups. One group is "Jacob," one is "Leah," and one is "Rachel." Groups discuss the following questions from the point of view of their character:

    a. How did you feel in the morning when Jacob realized he had been tricked and when Laban said: "It is not our custom for the younger daughter to marry before the older daughter"?

    b. Was it fair that Laban tricked Jacob into marrying Leah when he made a deal to marry Rachel?

    c. Did Jacob deserve the trick played on him?

2. Come back together as a class. Give each group a chance to report their responses. Read **Wisdom Weavers** on page 92.

3. Discuss: How does dishonesty lead to more dishonesty?

> **Wrapping It Up:** (5 minutes)
> Discuss: Jacob is in a cycle of dishonesty and mistrust. How can he work to fix it and stop the cycle from now on? *(Change his pattern of behavior, be open with people, behave with* derech eretz.*)* Note that it took Jacob many years to really learn this lesson, but in the next chapter we will see that he returns to his brother and acts differently.

CHAPTER 12 JACOB'S STRUGGLE
Lesson 1

Essential Question: What does it mean to "struggle with God"?

Lesson Objectives Students will:
1. Explain the origin of the name Israel.
2. Define several possibilities as to the identity of the mysterious stranger who wrestled with Jacob.
3. Understand that we are called the People of Israel because like Jacob/Israel, we are people who struggle with God by asking hard questions and learning new answers throughout our lives.

Getting Started: (5 minutes)
Ask students what their names mean. This was a homework assignment in chapter 10, so some of them will know.

Exploring the Text: (10-15 minutes)
1. Dramatic reading. Assign parts for Jacob, messengers, and a narrator to read pages 95-96.
2. **Compass**, page 96. Discuss: What do you think is going to happen next?
3. See Experiential Learning, below. After doing the experiential learning piece, students read the rest of the chapter on page 99 individually.
4. Those who end early should complete page 101.

Experiential Learning: (10-15 minutes)
1. In small groups of three, read the story of Jacob and the stranger on page 97. In each group, one person reads as the narrator, one as Jacob, and one as the stranger.
2. Read **Midrash Maker** on page 98 together. Point out that Israel means "one who struggles with God," which is one reason that the midrash suggests that the mysterious stranger was God.
3. Each student answers the questions on page 98 in his/her own book. Was the mysterious stranger Jacob's angel? Esau's angel? Jacob's conscience? God? Someone else? Take a class vote.

> **Wrapping It Up:** (10 minutes)
> Read and discuss **Word Wizard**, page 97. Emphasize the final two sentences. What does it mean that Jacob/Israel now "struggles with God"? Why do you think we are called the People of Israel? *(Answers will and should vary, but one concise way to explain it is that like Jacob, we are people who struggle with God by asking hard questions and learning new answers throughout our lives. Like many questions in the Torah, these questions defy easy answer and allow for an evolving response. Students can understand the idea of a question with answers that grow as we grow.)*

CHAPTER 13 THE DREAMER
Lesson 1

Essential Question: Was Jacob right in giving Joseph the *k'tonet pasim*?

Lesson Objectives Students will be able to:
1. Compare examples of jealousy between siblings in the Torah.
2. Recognize the results of Jacob's favoritism towards Joseph.
3. Define the term *k'tonet pasim*.

Getting Started/The Tech Connection: (10 minutes)
1. Assign half the students to the available computers. Individually or in pairs, students take the sibling rivalry quiz found at http://www.babaganewz.com/quizzes/sibling-rivalry-how-sweet-are-you.
2. With the other half of the class, review the beginning of the story of Cain and Abel (page 25) and the story of Jacob and Esau (pages 78 and 82). Explain that in this story we will see more jealousy and conflict between siblings.
3. Switch groups.
4. If there are not enough available computers, print the quiz for students to complete in writing. To score: Take the quiz yourself three times online, being careful to indicate the same types of answers each time and print the three different possible conclusions. It will not be difficult to look at the each student's responses and see which category s/he best fits.

Exploring the Text:
1. (10 minutes) Volunteers read page 103 and the **Word Wizard** on page 104. Make sure everyone understands what a *k'tonet pasim* (colorful coat) is. Allow time for students to consider and write down their thoughts about the **Word Wizard** question, "Was Jacob right in giving Joseph the *k'tonet pasim*?"
2. (10 minutes) In pairs, students read the two paragraphs on page 105 and discuss the two **compass** questions. Each pair writes answers to the questions. Collect the responses or walk around checking what they wrote.
3. (10 minutes) Students complete the chapter reading individually. Those who finish should do **Time Traveler** page 107 and **Say it Again** page 109.

Experiential Learning: (10 minutes)
Bring in a collection of magazines and newspapers for students to design a *k'tonet pasim* filled with symbols from Joseph's life or from Jacob's life. *(Examples may include a ladder, angels, facial expressions of Joseph's brothers, etc.)*

> **Wrapping It Up:** (5 minutes)
> Discuss as a class: Was Jacob right in giving Joseph the *k'tonet pasim*?

CHAPTER 14 JOSEPH'S GIFT
Lesson 1

Essential Question: How can we use our own gifts and talents towards *tikun olam*, making the world a better place?

Lesson Objectives Students will be able to:
1. Define what impressed Pharaoh about Joseph.
2. Describe how Joseph used his gifts towards *tikun olam*.
3. Explore how students can also be involved in *tikun olam*.

Getting Started: (3 minutes)
Introduce the idea of *tikun olam*, repairing the world, or making the world a better place. Explain that this is part of working as God's partner in the world and part of being created *b'tzelem Elohim*, in the image of God. Examples include working for justice, caring for the environment, and healing the sick.

Exploring the Text: (15 minutes)
Give each student (or pair of students) a section of the story to read. After a couple of minutes, ask each student to summarize his or her section, so that the class hears the whole story. Be prepared to add details if necessary.

Experiential Learning: (30 minutes)
Groups complete the following activities, which do not have to be done in order, taking turns with the computers and the art materials.

1. **Time Traveler: Joseph's Life Story**, page 116. Number the pictures. *(Correct answers: 2,4,1,5,3.)*
2. **Midrash Maker: Joseph's New Job**, page 117. To be done in pairs or small groups.
3. **Wisdom Weavers: The Greatest Gift of All**, page 118. With a friend, read and share. Continue with **Share Your Gifts**, page 119. Use as written or see **Tech Connection** below.
4. Students create mobiles depicting images from Joseph's, Pharaoh's, and the butler's dreams in this chapter. Use materials such as yarn or string, pipe cleaners, cardboard or construction paper, markers or colored pencils, scissors, and a hole punch. Students cut out images from the dreams from cardboard or construction paper, such as sun, moon, and stars; bundles of grain; grape clusters; a cup; fat and skinny cows; and fat and skinny ears of corn. Students decorate the cutouts and then hang them from frames made of pipe cleaners.

The Tech Connection: Share Your Gifts, page 119
Instead of writing their gifts on the preprinted boxes, students design their gifts on the computer. Each student creates a page with his/her name and gift of a talent, skill, or ability. These can then be printed and compiled into a class book, or included on a class Web page online. This can be one of the stations above or done at home.

Wrapping It Up: (5 minutes)
Bring the class back together. Ask what they do in their lives towards *tikun olam*. Encourage every child to give an answer.

CHAPTER 15 JOSEPH'S FORGIVENESS
Lesson 1

Essential Question: Is it more important to be right or to forgive people who have done us wrong?

Lesson Objectives Students will be able to:
1. Explain Joseph's choice to forgive his brothers.
2. Discuss how we can follow Joseph's example of forgiving people who have hurt us.
3. Explain how Jacob's family settled in Egypt.

Getting Started: (6 minutes)
Review the story of Joseph so far. Who was Joseph's father and how did he treat Joseph? *(Jacob loved Joseph the best of all his sons because he was the son of his favorite wife, Rachel. Jacob favored him and bought him special presents, especially a* k'tonet pasim.*)* How did the other brothers react? *(They were jealous of Joseph because Jacob favored him and they were angry at Joseph because he dreamed that they would all bow down to him. They decided to get rid of him by throwing him in a pit and selling him into slavery.)* What happened to Joseph in Egypt? *(First he was a servant to Potiphar. Then he was in jail. Now he is the second in command to Pharaoh and he is in charge of all the food in Egypt.)*

Experiential Learning: (20-25 minutes)
1. Tell the students: Imagine that the famine is in Canaan, too, and Joseph's brothers are coming to Egypt to buy food. Joseph sees them. What do you think he should do? Take three to four answers.
2. Create a short list on the board in two columns, one labeled, "He should take revenge" and one labeled, "He should forgive them." Ask students to go to one side of the room if they think that Joseph should seek revenge and to the other side of the room if they think Joseph should forgive the brothers.

Allow five minutes for both groups to prepare a skit of what might happen, and ask each group to perform its skit. Give students the opportunity to switch groups if they wish.

Exploring the Text:
1. (10 minutes) While still sitting in their groups, students read the chapter individually. As they finish, students should complete page 127 and then form pairs and complete page 129 together.
2. (10 minutes) Ask: What did you think of what Joseph did? Discuss in the two groups. Each group should craft a reaction to Joseph's actions and share it with the other group.

> **Wrapping It Up:** (5 minutes)
> Tell students that when we finish a book of the Torah, we all stand up and say (Ḥazak, ḥazak, v'nitḥazek). This is the end of *Sefer Bereisheet*, Genesis. Call out random groups to practice saying this phrase; for example, anyone wearing boots today, anyone wearing a blue shirt, etc. Finally, the whole class stands up and says it together.

CHAPTER 16 BABY MOSES
Lesson 1

Essential Question: What can we do to help bring justice to the world for Jews and others?

Lesson Objectives Students will be able to:
1. Identify the women who did their part to help save the Israelite babies.
2. Relate to the midwives as the first example of civil disobedience and explain that the midwives may have been Hebrew women or may have been Egyptian women.
3. Define ways that Jews have been involved in bringing justice to the world.

Getting Started: (5 minutes)
Remind the students of the quiz they took about different kinds of courage, way back in chapter 7. Ask if anyone knows who Ruby Bridges was. If students know, let them tell the story. If not, tell the story of Ruby Bridges, the first black child to attend an all-white public school in the South in 1960.

Exploring the Text: (10 minutes)
Students read the story individually. While they are reading, they underline or highlight every woman who helped save the life of Baby Moses. *(Midwives, Yocheved, Miriam, Pharaoh's daughter.)*

Experiential Learning: (20 minutes)
1. A group of students acts out the section of the story involving the midwives in Exodus 1:11-22 on pages 131-132.
2. After the skit, write on the board: הַמְיַלְדוֹת הָעִבְרִיּוֹת (*hamiyaldot haivriot*)—"the Hebrew midwives." Ask for two possible meanings *(Hebrew women who are midwives or midwives to the Hebrew women.)*
3. In the skit, were the midwives portrayed as Hebrew women or Egyptian women?
4. If students say "Hebrew women," relate that the famous commentator Rashi says that the midwives were actually Miriam and Yocheved.
    b. If students say "Egyptian women," ask what would make Egyptian women risk Pharaoh's anger for the sake of the Hebrews. *(Answers might include: they were acting b'tzelem Elohim; midwives are about bringing live babies into the world, not about killing babies; maybe they did not care what kind of women and babies they were helping.)*
    c. Explain that the Torah relates that these midwives believed in God's rules for the world more than in Pharaoh's rules for the world. They were engaging in what we call civil disobedience, which means breaking a law in a peaceful way because of a belief that the law is wrong.
4. Students write a poem or song about or in the words of one of the women in this chapter.

Tech Connection: (10 minutes)
Go to http://www.babaganewz.com/values/justice and read one of the stories about Jews who are involved in justice in the world. Continue this discussion with parents at home.

> **Wrapping It Up:** (10 minutes)
> What are some examples of Jews who work for justice in the world?

The Explorer's Bible Volume I • Teacher's Lesson Plan Manual

CHAPTER 17 MOSES STANDS BEFORE GOD
Lesson 1

Essential Question: How is the God of Abraham, the God of Isaac, the God of Jacob, also the God of each one of us?

Lesson Objectives Students will be able to:
1. Identify significant experiences in the life of Moses.
2. Explain the importance of the phrase in the Amidah: "God of Abraham, God of Isaac, God of Jacob."
3. Begin to explore their own relationship with God.

Getting Started: (3 minutes)
Look at the picture on pages 138 and 139. Ask students to describe what they see. Ask: What do you see on this tree besides flames? *(Leaves.)* Why is this remarkable? *(Flames would normally burn off the leaves.)* What do you think this unusual fire might mean? Who else saw it? *(Moses.)*

Exploring the Text: (20 minutes)
1. A volunteer reads Exodus 2:11-12 on page 139 aloud.
2. Assign students to play the parts of narrator, Moses, and slave for a dramatic reading of Exodus 2:13-15 on page 140. After the dramatic reading, students complete the **Word Wizard** in pairs.
3. Students silently read Exodus 2:15-25 on page 141 and complete the top **Compass**. When students finish, ask them to go back in the book and find God's covenant with Abraham *(page 45)*.
4. Assign students to play the parts of narrator, God, and Moses for a dramatic reading of Exodus 3:1-6 on page 141.
5. Look at the picture on page 143. Ask: What kinds of work are the slaves doing?
6. Continue dramatic reading of Exodus 3:7-12 on page 142 with different volunteers. Ask: What do you think God means when God says to Moses: "I will be with you"?
7. Continue dramatic reading of Exodus 4:1-5 page 142 and Exodus 4:10-18 page 144 with different volunteers.

Experiential Learning: (15 minutes)
1. Pairs do **Midrash Maker** on page 145.
2. Students individually complete **It's No Excuse**, page 147. Make sure they understand that their thought bubbles should restate the original thought bubbles.
3. Point out that God makes sure that Moses knows he is speaking to "the God of Abraham, the God of Isaac, and the God of Jacob." Explain that we refer to God in the same way at the beginning of the Amidah prayer. Have students open their *siddurim* to the Amidah. If you are comfortable with it, give it out *Tanachim* and let them compare the Hebrew in Exodus 3:15. Ask: Why do you think God used these words with Moses and why do we use them today? *(To remember our connection to our ancestors.)*
4. Tell students that many congregations add to the Amidah: "God of Sarah, God of Rebecca, God of Rachel, and God of Leah." Ask if they like that addition.

Wrapping It Up: (5 minutes)
Ask: Why do we say, "God of Abraham, God of Isaac, God of Jacob" rather than just simply, "God of Abraham, Isaac and Jacob"? *(Because it is repeating the way the passage is phrased in the Torah; to teach us that each person experiences God in his or her own way; to remind us that God is with each one of us as rise to the challenges in our lives.)*

CHAPTER 18 FREEDOM AND THE FUTURE
Lesson 1

Essential Question: Why do we observe Passover?

Lesson Objectives Students will be able to:
1. Explain the story of the ten plagues.
2. Relate the Exodus to the celebration of Pesaḥ.
3. Describe the benefits of working together as a community.

Getting Started: (5 minutes)
Students list five activities they like to do. Which of those things could you do if you were a slave? List them on the board. (See **Compass**, page 149.)

Exploring the Text: (15 minutes)
1. A volunteer reads Exodus 5:1-6:1 on page 149. How do you think the slaves felt when they heard that they would be required to find straw to make bricks while maintaining the same number of bricks as before?
2. Volunteer reads Exodus 7:10-13 on page 150. Do you think the trick with the staff and the serpent convinced the Egyptians to believe in God? *(Probably not, since the Egyptian magicians could do the same thing.)*
3. Assign one to two students to read each plague. Students silently read the section of the chapter that contains "their" plague *(First plague, blood, 7:19-22; second plague, frogs, 8:1-2 & 4-11; third plague, lice; fourth plague, swarms of insects; fifth plague, cattle disease; and sixth plague, boils, 8:12-9:12; seventh plague, hail, 9:18-35; eighth plague, locusts, 10:4-20; ninth plague, darkness, 10:21-27; tenth plague, death of the firstborn, 11:1-6 & 12:30-34.)* Call out the plague number, and students who read that plague announce and explain it.
4. Teacher reads page 154 out loud.
5. Students complete **Time Traveler** on page 155 individually.

Experiential Learning: (20 minutes)
1. Divide students into groups of those who want to:

    a. Write a rap of what the slaves might have said to Moses when they heard that they have to find straw to make bricks while maintaining the same quota as before.

    b. Write a rap about the ten plagues.

    c. Write a rap about putting the blood on the doorposts and leaving Egypt.

    d. Write a rap about celebrating Pesaḥ today.

2. Groups perform their raps for the others.
3. Collect the raps and combine them into one class rap. If the timing works out, send it home for use at students' family *s'darim*.

Wrapping It Up: (5 minutes)
Read **Wisdom Weavers** together on page 156.

Chapter 18: Lesson 2

Essential Question: How is putting a mezuzah on our doorpost a choice that marks us as part of the Jewish community?

Lesson Objectives Students will be able to:
1. Explain the significance of the mezuzah.
2. Connect the mezuzah both to the Pesaḥ story and to the Sh'ma.
3. Understand how having a mezuzah is a sign of being part of the Jewish community.

Getting Started: (5 minutes)
Sing the class rap written in the previous class.

Exploring the Text: (5 minutes)
A volunteer reads Exodus 12:1-27 on page 153. Ask: Blood on the doorposts reminds you of what mitzvah that we do today? *(Affixing mezuzot.)*

Experiential Learning: (15 minutes)
1. Students open their *siddurim* and read the first paragraph of the Sh'ma in Hebrew. Ask: Where in the Sh'ma does it tell us to put *mezuzot* on our doorposts? *(The very last line of the v'ahavtah paragraph.)* Ask: Why do we put *mezuzot* on our doorposts? *(To show that we have a Jewish house; to remind us when we come into the house that we have a Jewish house; to remind us when we leave that house that we are Jews and should behave accordingly.)*
2. If possible, show students what a mezuzah parchment looks and feels like. Turn it over and ask what they notice on the back. They will be able to feel the softness of the animal skin, and they will see that there are three Hebrew letters written on the back, *shin, dalet, yud*, which spells Shadai, one of the names of God. The mezuzah is rolled so that the Shadai shows. Often mezuzah cases include that particular name for God or just the letter *shin* as a reminder.
3. There is room here to elaborate, if you choose. For example, *mezuzot*, tefillin, and Torah scrolls are all written on parchment, with a special quill, by a scribe called a *sofer*.
4. Discuss how having a mezuzah on the door is a sign of being part of the Jewish community.

Tech Connection: (15 minutes)
1. Go to http://www.youtube.com/watch?v=zZ5dk656t1s&feature=related and watch the *soferet* Julie Seltzer write a Torah.
2. Go to http://www.babaganewz.com/search/node/mezuzah, click on any of the links, read and enjoy!

Wrapping It Up: (10 minutes)
Take a walk around the synagogue building and look at different *mezuzot*.

Assessment, Reinforcement, and Review

From time to time, teachers should devote a lesson to reviewing and reinforcing what has been learned. This is also a good opportunity to assess the students' retention. Below you will find some suggestions for games, puzzles, and quizzes to begin the review process; expansion and variation will be needed as you use the ideas on different occasions. These suggestions focus on reviewing characters and events as well as ethical concepts and terms.

As the year progresses and the students get farther along in the book, you will be able to incorporate more and more examples into your games, puzzles, and quizzes. Activities should be organized to maximize participation among all students.

The following may be used for an oral game, perhaps in teams: Who am I?
1. After I listened to the snake, I ate from the Tree of Knowledge. *(Eve)*
2. I said: "Am I my brother's keeper?" *(Cain)*
3. The rest of the world was corrupt, but I walked with God. *(Noah)*
4. I argued with God, saying: "Should not the Judge of all the earth act justly?" *(Abraham)*
5. When I died, my husband bought a burial plot for me. *(Sarah)*
6. I schlepped water for a stranger and all his camels. *(Rebecca)*
7. My brother bought my birthright and stole my blessing. *(Esau)*
8. I had 12 sons and one daughter. *(Jacob)*
9. My father made me a *k'tonet pasim* and my brothers were so jealous. *(Joseph)*
10. I forgave my brothers for selling me into slavery in Egypt. *(Joseph)*

Written quiz: Match the dream to the dreamer:
1. A ladder with angels going up and down *(Jacob)*
2. The sun and moon and stars bowed to me *(Joseph)*
3. I squeezed grapes into a wine cup and I gave the cup to Pharaoh *(the butler)*
4. Seven skinny cows ate seven fat cows—and stayed skinny! *(Pharaoh)*

Written or oral: Define or explain the mitzvah and match it to the appropriate Torah character or characters:
1. *Hachnasat orḥim* (welcoming guests) *(Abraham, Sarah, Lot, Rebecca)*
2. Taking care of animals *(Noah, Rebecca)*
3. Standing up for justice *(Abraham, Lot, Moses)*

Written exercise: Explain the following terms and give an example of how it applies to your life:
1. *B'tzelem Elohim (in the image of God)*
2. *Derech eretz (basic moral behavior)*
3. *Tzedek/mishpat (justice)*
4. Being our brothers' keepers *(having responsibility for others)*
5. *Tikun olam (working to improve the world)*
6. *Hachnasat orḥim (welcoming guests)*

Other games and quizzes may include: Match the couples *(Adam/Eve; Abraham/Sarah; Isaac/Rebecca; Jacob/Rachel/Leah; Yocheved/Amram; Moses/Zipporah)*, match the siblings: *(Cain/Abel; Jacob/Esau; Judah/Joseph; Moses/Miriam/Aaron)*, and match the item to the character *(Tree of Knowledge-Adam/Eve; ark-Noah; tent-Abraham/Sarah; staff-Moses)*.

www.ingramcontent.com/pod-product-compliance
Lightning Source LLC
Chambersburg PA
CBHW081220230426
43666CB00015B/2828